30 Minutes of Laughter

of Laughter

and a few minutes of FEAR

stories by Leonard Bilski

Owner of

Emergency

Environmental Control

LifeRich Publishing is a registered trademark of The Reader's Digest Association, Inc.

LifeRich Publishing books may be ordered through booksellers or by contacting:

LifeRich Publishing
1663 Liberty Drive
Bloomington, IN 47403
www.liferichpublishing.com
1 (888) 238-8637

ISBN: 978-1-4897-0840-3 (sc)
ISBN: 978-1-4897-0839-7 (e)

Library of Congress Control Number: 2016908805

Print information available on the last page.

LifeRich Publishing rev. date: 06/27/2016

30 Minutes Laughter

and a few minutes of FEAR

Stories by

Leonard Bilski

Owner of

Emergency Environmental Control

516-983-7910

Photos by

Lily Hofmann

Pics

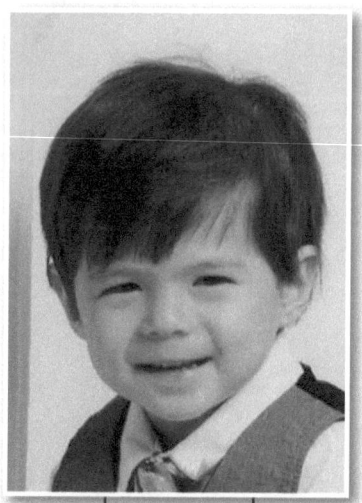

1st Son

Leonard W. Bilski, Sr.
Leonard W. Bilski, Jr.

Leonard W. Bilski, Sr.
Age 66

My Mom & Step Dad
Claire & Mike Grace

Understanding the Author

My mother and father divorced when I was 3 years old! My father, Leonard W. Bilski Sr., was an alcoholic and a functional schizophrenic! He worked in Queens for the United States Post Office. Mom, dad and I lived with my dad's mom who was wealthy. After my parents divorced, dad continued to live at his mothers house. I would visit my dad every 2 weeks. I would arrive on Friday after school and stay with him through Sunday.

My visits with dad were great. He bought me anything and his mom bought me everything else I wanted. During these visits I would have to go to the bar with my dad where he would drink for hours and hours. I would be playing arcade games while he drank. He drank to the point of falling down at times. My father would scare me by claiming people were chasing us. I remember when I was between the ages of 5-11, dad would carry a gun or a knife. He felt those weapons would keep us safe from the people who were chasing us. In the many hours I spent with my dad, he would tell me over and over and over again that men don't cry, men don't back out of fights and that men were TOUGH! Hour after hour he would drive those thoughts into me while speeding and being chased. My dad would take me to Rockaway Playland a lot. He continued his work with the post office until being diagnosed Schizophrenic. For years he collected disability money. So I grew up believing that alcohol, fighting and a sharp stern way of speaking were normal. I was told hourly that men are strong, men feel no pain and that men make tough decisions, meaning no feminine ways.

My mom remarried. I lived with her and my step dad. They were always arguing over money, bills and being broke. My mother would get food stamps and a 20 pound log of cheese provided by the state. We were poor. I had clothes handed down to me and other cheap clothes. I still remember a pair of purple suede sneakers I had to wear to 6th grade. I was fat from eating all the government cheese and my hair was greasy. All the kids would tease me. Because we were so poor, I began hustling. I would work for tips by carrying Christmas trees from the lot for people who bought them. I would go to the supermarket and carry packages for tips there as well. Because kids were teasing me at school, I began to fight and got a reputation as a tough guy. As I began high school, my thoughts about life were full of confusion. I became involved with boxing, hustling money, a landscaping company and an exterminating company. I ended up serving 3 years in prison for a non-violent crime. I had obsessions in life; weight, eating, dieting, sex, money, fighting and boxing. I have 4 children with 3 different women. I have been with Lily for 11 years and have 2 children with her.

In my years boxing, I won the 1988 Empire State Games and trained in heavy weight champion Larry Holmes' boxing camp. In 1991 I boxed and received a brain injury, water on the brain, causing a stroke to affect one side of my body. Other affects of this injury caused my eyes to become crossed and a weakening limp when I walk. Doctors have said I might have to be in a wheelchair years from now. In 2008, over 17 years later, I had surgery to reattach my crossed eyes. The success of the surgery gave me the incentive to lose 70 lbs. I was 240 lbs. when I decided to lose some weight. I then went on to fight in 4 New York State registered boxing matches at 160 lbs and 43 years old. After that I had 3 car accidents, needed 2 spine surgeries, dropped a 33 foot ladder on my toe and had to have the bone removed. Most recently I had my ear almost sliced off.

I still climb onto roofs for wild life and pest control. I have many physical issues but I never give up on anything. I will always work no matter what condition I may be in. I sometimes am haunted by thoughts that were ingrained in me from childhood. Day by day I am learning to overcome the negativity of those thoughts by practicing a healthy positive outlook.

I hope you have a better understanding of why my thoughts in life are the way they are. Thank you for reading my book and I hope to have it in stores soon!

Life's Obstacles!

Injuries, disabilities, poverty, insecurities, problems, family, no family. Remember... whatever your problem is always remember that your actions draw a positive or negative affect. Most of the time you have the power to make decisions in the way life turns out. NEVER give up and always keep trying. At times in my life, I have wondered who was holding the voodoo doll on me. Look at all my physical, mental and emotional obstacles! Yet I still smile and try to overcome all!

Thanks again for reading.

Leonard Bilski, Jr.
Author and Writer

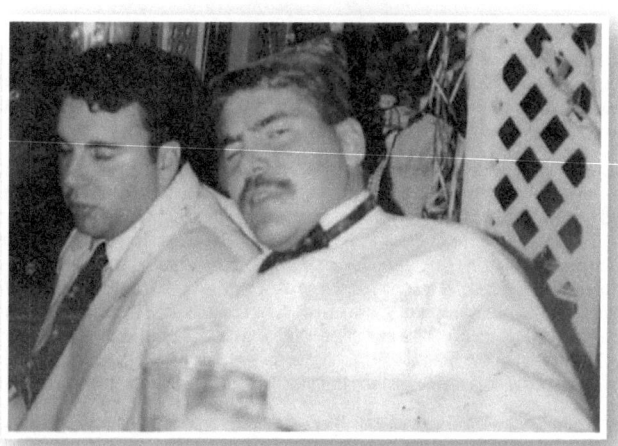

Larry Holmes - 1988 @ his boxing camp

2

Larry Holmes Enterprises, Inc.

Leonard Bilski

January 22, 2016

Dear Mr. Bilski:

This letter will serve as permission to use the 1988 picture taken at my training center in your book, 30 Minutes of Laughter.

Regards,

Larry Holmes

Charles E. Wynn

COMMONWEALTH OF PENNSYLVANIA
NOTARIAL SEAL
CHARLES E. WYNN, Notary Public
City of Easton, Northampton County
My Commission Expires April 26, 2016

L & D Holmes Plaza, 91 Larry Holmes Drive • Easton, PA 18042 • Phone (610) 253-6905 • FAX (610) 253-0652

Flying Squirrel

I went to a house and a lady had squirrels running in her house. They were baby flying squirrels, so cute. They must have been hungry; they ran right up to me, cute like a squirrel with a beaver like tail, colored like a brown skunk. So I pet the head of one of the three, he put his tail up and down like a dog. I was so excited to tell my wife and my kids. I brought them home and spent $300 on a tank, heaters and covers. The kids named him Alvin, He squeeked and danced like Happy Feet when a Family member approached. I bought this cozy little bed for him to sleep in and he spends all his

Flying Squirrel

time in it. How cute, until three days later, he never woke up. My wife reads up on flying squirrels and found out the he died from the material that was in the bed he loved. The kids were crying, my wife yelled at me - "why did I get the kids so hooked on them?" So I tell them I have plenty of flying squirrel jobs.

We researched the food they needed. So now all I need is a flying squirrel. I caught one but he's older, yet friendly. I rubbed his nose a few times and threw him in a cage. So here we go. I take them out of the cage and I pet his nose. He waits, and then lunges. His teeth, cute as a beaver, yet they go through the middle of my finger and out the other side. The pain is awful. I scream and my wife and kids are locked in fear. I pull and he will not release my finger. I run swinging my hand back and forth over and over until finally he shot like a rubber band into the air. My finger was swollen for three weeks. I busted and threw out the tank. I said "Sorry kids, but no squirrel".

Birds

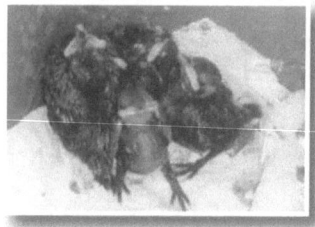

Usually you have to humanely kill most animals and birds when you catch them. I like to release what I can. I tell people when they ask, what do you do with them, I see that they go into the Witness Protection Program. I cannot tell you, But they are fine. So I went in the hole in the gutter that sparrows like. I stuck my hand in and grabbed them. I took them out and humanely eliminate them unfortunately.

I grabbed one one day and he was so cute. Every word I said he would chirp back. If I said nothing, he said nothing. So I brought this one home and we researched how to feed him. Eventually my Wife and kids are up feeding birds, all day and night, trying to nurse them to strength and health. Most people are trying to get rid of these things from their windows and attic and here I am taking them home. Now I am doing

bird jobs every day. We had about 18 baby birds at one time. They thought we were family jumping in all of our hands and playing with the cat. Now after 2 months of feeding,

Birds

they were flying around the house, a collection of live wild birds. As I come home they would land on my arms and shoulders. If I put my arms out, they came like a pet to my hands. I felt like Snow White.

After a while it was ridiculous. As they were learning to fly, they were conducting their practice from the ceiling fan to the blinds on the wall while peeing and pooping everywhere. My dogs were going nuts trying to get them. It's a big problem. The house stinks. The birds are big now. We must let them go. So we put them on the deck. They flew back to me, back to the tree. I set food and water bowls on the deck. My neighbor who can't stand me is looking off her deck at me. All of a sudden the birds from the tree start flying to her landing and getting in her hair. She is screaming. They kept bouncing off her thinking she was my wife. I had to go over and explain. It was so funny. It was like a scene from the movie "The Birds".

Skunk

I never saw a skunk ever. But I got referred to a skunk problem. The job was two hours from my office. It was slow. So I'll try it. I read that they like cat food. I'm off. I get the cages, and I set up the job. The next day I slowly walk up as I catch sight of my first skunk in a cage. As in cartoons, I think the tail will point at me and shoot me. Think of a person fainting all of a sudden. It stinks and you see nothing. It was like a gas chamber. The smell was everywhere. On my third day and sixth skunk I figure out if you hold the cage to the side of you, I have no smell or gas release. So I walk slowly to a cage. I saw a skunk with his tail aimed at me. He's staring at me like a cartoon character, moving his head from my feet to my head, up and down. No one else is with me. I laugh out loud. I say, what are you doing? I'm about fifteen feet away and all of a sudden - his butt turns into a huge hole - gross! It looked like an upside down toilet plunger. I yelled to myself-Eew.... The smell hits me like a tornado - horrible! I pack him in the truck. I was two hours from home, but I got a call. I caught two squirrels in the town of Armonk, a huge million dollar house. I knocked on the door. The lady opened the door and I stepped inside. She screamed at the daughter, I told you to wash the dogs butt. She says it's not the dog that smells.

At the same time they stared at me with angry frowns. I said, I am so sorry I have a skunk in the truck. They're angry, but I must get the animals out of the attic. How embarrassing!

Bees 1

"I have bees in a daycare. Can you come?"

I get there but there are 15 kids 6 to 8 years old all around. She says you have to move all of the toys before you spray. Now, we are talking toys, toys, toys all over. I said okay. I was starting to see a bee here and there. All the kids were watching me. All of a sudden I pulled a toy and shazam, 500 bees zap, sting. The bees' nest was attached to the toy. The lady must not have needed that toy in weeks. I started screaming, cursing, yelling, running zig zagging around the yard. I glanced at the kids who were terrified shaking. I then screamed and began smacking on my body. I was furious with this lady. She never told me they were in the toy. The poor kids' faces. I don't think they will ever forget me or the bees.

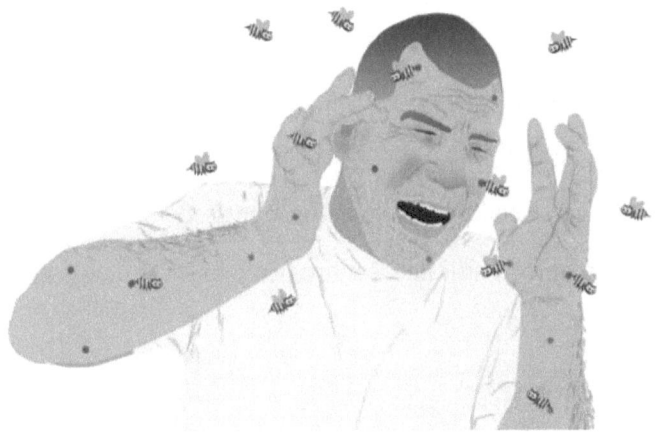

Bees 2

I have been doing pest control since I was 18. I had purchased an expensive bee suit. I went up the ladder and somehow the bees got in my neck opening, sting, sting, sting. I almost went down the ladder. I never wore a bee suit again.

I got a call about a three foot wide bees nest up a tree. I put a ladder leaning on a branch. I sprayed pesticide and the bees were dropping like hail. Everyone was telling me I'm crazy. They had video cameras, no big deal to me. 500$ for the job. So, I'm laughing on my way to the next bee job. I arrive and the lady stood next to me. She said there were hornets under that cushion. The lady was two feet from me. I pointed at the cushion and asked over there? All of a sudden the bees speak English. I was on the porch and a dark black line of bees started coming at me. Sting, sting, sting, buzz. I started to scream and run. The entire bees' nest was following me. I was stung 40 or so times on my face, my mouth, my eyes, my arms. and my legs. I looked like a deformed elephant man. I drove to the pharmacy to get Benadryl as everyone begged me to go to the hospital. I explained I still had 2 more bee jobs. The Lady was not stung.

Bats

The phone rings and a girl asks if I can help her with a bat that is in her one year old child's room. Off I go on another emergency for the wildlife & bug man. I get there and she is in tears. I see the bat wedged in between the stucco paint in the ceiling. Remember in the 70's, all the Grandmas felt that if you dip the paint brush in the paint and dab it you had a special look. When it dried you had points of paint on the wall and ceiling. I set a three foot A-frame ladder under the bat. I stayed as quiet as can be. Vibration or noise may make him move. I had a short sleeve shirt on. I got a 24 inch glue board, got close and swung and missed him. But the glue board slammed onto my hairy gorilla-like arm. It was stuck like crazy glue. I try to gently pull it off, oww! It was no joke. Any pulling and it pulled my hair. So I yank hard and then I'm sporting an arm with bald patches. I was furious. I look at the bat with anger. He did it to me. I was wild with anger. I set up again and slam I hit the bat, but I also hit the ceiling. The 24 inch glue board was stuck on the bat but also on the ceiling. For twenty minutes I try to get it off. It finally came off but so did 15 inches of the stucco ceiling. Now there is a huge hole in the ceiling. I was paid, never said a word and left.

Bats in the Roof

A construction crew was doing a job at a house and they couldn't remove the gutter as the bats were in it. They called their exterminator and he says, we've got a guy who does anything. Three companies refer me to any dangerous jobs. I do it all. I did not go to college. So I got to the house and the workers pointed to the roof. I climbed up and banged the gutter with a hammer and one bat came out. The workers complained I was not in the correct spot. So I moved over about 3 feet. The contractor was holding the bottom of the ladder. Bang, bang, all of a sudden bats started flying out of the hole bouncing off my chest. My head, my arm, sticking, clinging to me. I was swinging my hands, yelling, making noises. Meanwhile, as bats flew out, they hit me, then swooped to the ground, 30,40, 50 bats. Everyone was yelling and watching me not holding the ladder. Some were laughing at me. The others were running as the bats swooped close to them. As I got down, one bat was still stuck to my arm and one to my thigh.

Bats in the Roof

When I got home my wife said "what happened to you." She was three months pregnant with our baby, so she got on the computer. She says I have rabies. She read online that I came in contact with bats and I will give rabies to her and the baby. I could care less about myself. But off to the emergency room we go. I filled out papers and they wanted to give me 3 - 10 inch needles in the stomach in each bite mark. As the needle went in the pain was so great the tears poured down my face. They told me I had to go back twice a week for shots for three months. When we were done I said see ya. **TELL YOUR KIDS TO GO TO COLLEGE.**

THESE STORIES ARE MY JOB.

Owl

I answer my phone 24 hours a day to get all the work I can. About ten years ago we had a 17 inch snow storm. A call came in - now remember there was a 17 inch blizzard outside. He said there was a huge owl in his fireplace. Are you sure it's an owl I ask? I asked "What's it doing in your fireplace." He panicked as he realized I might not believe him. So I humored him. He gave me his name and I told him I had a friend in high school with that name. He said that's my brother. He sounded for real, but it can't be an owl.

I just drove two and half hours in the blizzard. When I got there, the man looked traumatized with fear. He pointed and said "He is trying to get out." I looked and holy cow! It was a freakin owl! I only see them in the zoo. So I told him $400. He said okay. I scanned the fireplace. I had purchased a $500 pair of gloves that animals can't bite through. I was bit by a squirrel a few weeks before this and wasn't taking any chances. I stuck my hand in and the owl was moving back and forth. All of a sudden I heard a loud screech. A second owl jumped through the flue and started clawing my glove and arm. I nearly had a heart attack (I felt as though I was) as he was biting my arm. I screamed, the guy screamed, the owl was screeching.

Owl

We were all a mess in fright, and I was moving to pull my arm out. I screamed at the guy "You didn't tell me there were two owls!" Both of us were terrified. He said he didn't know. I closed the chimney flue. I started again and grabbed the owl and put him in the squirrel cage. See Picture. Owls are a protected species.

Now the other owl flew back up into the fireplace. The owner, a nut job, made me go on the roof with 15 inches of snow to look down the fireplace or no pay. I went outside. The roof had 15 inches of snow. The second floor had a deck so the roof was only about eight feet off the deck. I put a six foot ladder up and shoveled the roof to the chimney. I looked down the open flue - no owl. I wiggled an extension cord down the chimney. Must have flown out. I got my $400 and left. I showed off the owl and then brought it to the animal hospital.

I no sooner got home than the guy calls that the other owl is back. Another two and a half hour drive and starting all over again.

Raccoon

Hello! So I am the only nut job that waits for work call 24 hours a day, like a bird looking for scraps. So a guy called me, yelling "Help! Help! A raccoon is trying to eat me. Hurry. Help!". So I said "Calm down". "Hurry, hurry!" he yelled.

I am familiar with the road he lived on, behind a 7-11 on 25 in Northport. I pulled on the block looking for the house - Pitch Black. The house number I believe it was had 1 bedroom light on. I got out, slammed my door. :Hello, Hello" I heard. I glanced over to the area of the sound, the room with the light on. "Hello, Hello". Then I saw a head pop up in the window then disappear, again and again. "Hello", the head up and down. Oh great I said to myself, 2am and another nut job. Why did I come?

Then I heard "The door is open". "Come in. Hurry! Help!". Well I already drove here I might as well look. So I slowly entered. I heard Bang, Smash, Pidda Patter. I was relieved, he must have something. So I walked into the kitchen and saw a huge hole next to the ceiling fan. I think he had a raccoon so I was not here for noth-ing. All of a sudden, charging in my direction, now I'm like the guy, he's coming at me. I jumped back. He scampered behind the couch. So I walked outside with no food, I will scare him into the traps I think. 30 minutes later and a few dramatic scampers and... Wala! I caught my raccoon. So "Time to go" I said to myself.

Raccoon

So I walked with the huge raccoon to the room at the end of the hallway. As I got closer I heard crying, so I knocked on the door...knock, knock, knock. The man yelled in a whining voice "NO NO NO, I am not coming out". Cry, cry, cry. "Hey Buddy" I said, "the raccoon is in the cage". "NO NO NO, not coming out" Now I was getting mad, I wasn't going to get paid. So I angrily took the cage and the raccoon outside. I walked back in, the man was still crying. "Come out" I told him. "Are you sure?" he asked. I banged on the door louder..."Yeah!".

He opened the door, tears, red. The man was about 60 years old and only 2 1/2 feet tall. The raccoon was as big as the man on back legs. I got paid and left. The poor man was short and senile so he could not reach the window.

Rats 1

I got a call from an old lady about 70 years old. Her other exterminator quit. She has a bad mouse problem. She made an appointment with me. She said the other exterminator would not go in the attic. I thought, what a baby. I started to crawl in insulation on my belly. All of a sudden, I heard a squeak. Then I heard a loud movement in the insulation. I thought, "that is no mouse". Quickly there was movement and noises. Rats - large rats - began jumping and landing and running all over my body. Never have I seen this. It was like being in a school of bluefish in the water. Rats were everywhere, squeaking, jumping, crawling. I was in fear of my life.

I had dreams of rats eating me for weeks.

It was a dramatic experience. I caught

30 huge rats over the next two

weeks at her house.

Rats 2 / Dr. Reynolds

I got a call that somebody was complaining that some items were opened in the kitchen. I arrived for an inspection equipped with traps, poison and cages. I did not see any evidence. The home-owner was annoyed and told me he didn't want poison, traps or cages. I ask what wanted me to do? He said you must do something to make my wife happy. I had thick one inch glue traps. If you have a mouse or a rat, it will catch it. If it is a squirrel, you will see hair in the trap. You live on the water, you could have any of them. He said, I have Forbes magazine coming over to take pictures of my house and to see this wallpaper. Beautiful isn't it? It was imported from Egypt. He says all the traps must be picked up in the morning. I said call me or you can pick them up. He only agreed to the large rat glue traps with peanut butter on it. I left.

I service restaurants 24 hours a day. I was at a diner work-ing at 2 am. I got three missed calls. I called the number and he an-swered. You have to get here; my wife and daughter are screaming and crying. There is a huge rat in the trap and he is chewing his own leg off. There is blood everywhere. I said pick it up and throw it out. He started hyperventilating, he was a wreck, and he screamed "I can't look at it!". Again I said to pick it up and throw it out. No! He was screaming at me. I said I was forty minutes away. Dr. Reynolds says he was calling a neighbor.

The neighbor arrived. The rat chewed it's leg off and it was still vibrating and moving on the ground, blood was everywhere. Now the rat was chewing the other leg. The neighbor walked in, threw up on the floor and ran out. He asked me where I was and I said fifteen minutes away. He says he was calling another neighbor. As I pulled up to the house he came outside and said nastily says to "leave". It's about 4am now. He woke another neighbor who came over with a shovel. The neighbor beat this huge rat with a shovel so many times the blood stained and splattered all over the kitchen and the wallpaper. He said his wife plans to sue me and go to court, what a nightmare they were.

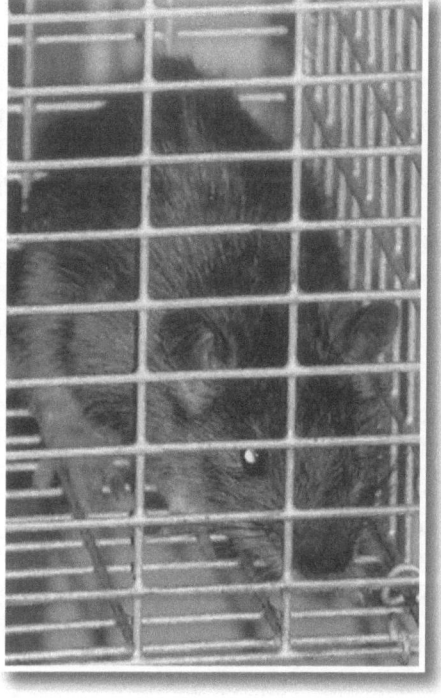

Squirrel

I got a call about 3am, "I have a squirrel on my bed". At this time I could grab a squirrel bare hands, my anger would direct to the squirrel. So I drove to the house. It was a beautiful house. The lady handed me baggies for my feet, like I was prepping for surgery, "okay" I thought. Then she argued price from $575 down to $400. She quietly walked me to the room and explained that the room was a "show room". All items in the room were expensive crystals, picture, vases, and a bed. The room was out of the ordinary, Big $$$ in that room. "There" she pointed at a squirrel tucked cozy on the bed snuggled in the bedspread. So I walked out and got a few cages and a few glue traps and set them against the wall. Now I must go at the squirrel. He bolts. I heard smash, smash, ding, ting. He smashed vases, statues, pictures before he hid. To find him, I needed to set all cages, traps and try to scare him and hope he would go in the traps. Well I ran, chased and tried everything to get him. It was summer and there was no air in this room, I was soaked in sweat. You could ring out my underwear - 2 cups of water.

It was hours and this room got destroyed. This was a wild animal on the loose running for his dear life with an angry man chasing him. I tried it all... No luck. I gave up. The squirrel found a hiding place and I could not find him. They begged me "Please, please, we will find him". So as they entered the room.... screams, tears, yelling. "What did you do to the room? What? Why?".

So I explained, "Hey lady, what did you think it was here? Kiddy Kiddy? It's a wild <u>animal</u>! So as I was talking, the squirrel ran out between us and out into the master bedroom. The husband ran

after him and I stayed put getting screamed at by the daughter and mother. The husband yelled "Get in here! Look! Look!". As I ran in the door my first sight were the hugest boots I had ever seen, bigger than a circus clowns boots. I said "Forget the squirrel, what dinosaur wears those boots?". I was in shock. He yelled "Get the squirrel!" I was out of ideas to capture the squirrel. I yelled "Hit it with the Boot!". Size 18 boots I was told - Huge. He angrily hit it with the boot. He knocked it out. Seeing my chance, I dived onto it, bare handed, choking it, not releasing. It woke up and started digging its teeth into my fingers. With blood pouring everywhere I yelled "Get me the glue paper, quick!" I wouldn't release it.

The husband handed me the glue board. With blood all over I remove one hand, still choking with the other, I still had him against the floor. I put the glue board over him on the floor. I banged him with my hand, but he was slowly getting away. I grabbed my flashlight and banged 3 times, until there is no more movement. The lady screamed "Oh NO, Oh No! Is he dead?". I picked the glue board up as the squirrel hang to it, "Hey lady, does he look dead?". She cried "Your ad said safe and humane pest control". I said "The first 2 hours were safe and humane pest control."

The lady called the police and I explained when they arrived that it bit me and I was chasing it for 3 hours. They said Okay. As I angrily pulled away in the car, I dialed the customers phone. "Hey lady! Look on your roof. You have two squirrels chewing through the roof. Everyone inside came running out of the house frantically.

Squirrel

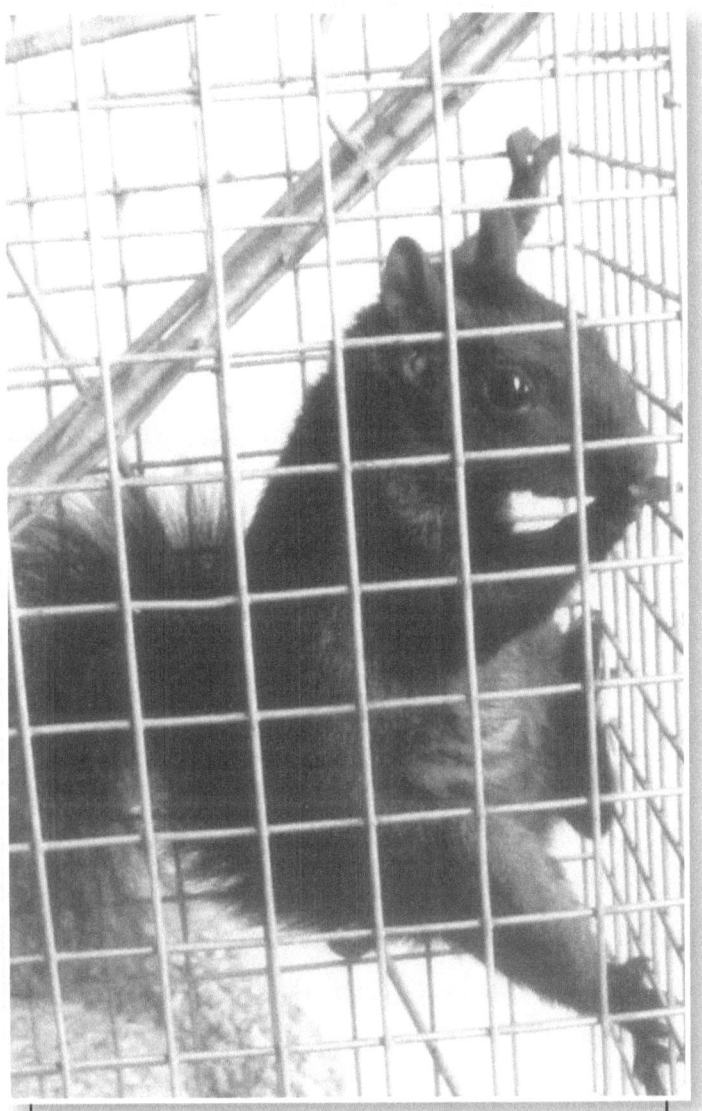

Yeah Yeah... Thats right I'm black. I'm a Black Squirrel!
Are you Prejudice?

Who Loves Buffet?

When you go to a buffet all you can eat for $14.99, crab legs, shrimp, spare ribs, etc. it is paradise for your belly. Do you notice that you always take more than you can eat? How about after you take three bites of food, are you aware the staff is already asking to take the plate. Think about it. How can they stay in business? It's like this. I will tell you about three buffets I service, but not all of them.

Now my plate was snatched quick so I got another plate again and again. I service their pest control at night when they are closed. I witnessed over 100 plates with food half piled on their plates. Four workers were going through the food trimming the chewed edges making the pieces you spit out look edible for the next day's lunch. They put all the food they salvage back in the food containers. I guess for lunch, so enjoy your buffet meal.

I have been doing pest control for thirty years. I've seen it all. In the kitchen of a restaurant over 100 degrees men are saturated with sweat. They are supposed to wear gloves and a hat. Let's be real. There is no AC in the kitchen. The people who work in the kitchen are not getting good pay. When an inspector enters the restaurant, by the time he gets in the kitchen everyone is perfectly in gloves, hat, etc. As you eat your spare ribs or your chicken, just think of who's dirty hands touched it. Many

Who Loves Buffet?

of the ribs, chicken, fried rice, all sit in open containers soaking in sauces or just sitting, flies or roaches crawl in, on, all over it. I see it weekly. They just brush it off and cook it, I guess the sweat of the workers or the feces of the rodents blend in with the sauce.

I exterminated a restaurant in Jericho, NY. This guy was 72, still working the kitchen. He was so cheap. He never used an exterminator until it was so bad that he had to. Then the $, forget it. You would take his wife on a date easier than getting money out of him. He had huge rats. I told him $350. The only way he agreed is if I played cards for money. I went into the kitchen, set up traps all over, and then came out to the card game. They were talking in different languages and I was losing all my money. All of a sudden we heard snap, snap, snap and a cry and we looked up. I walked inside, three huge rats. The owner was so pissed that I charged $350, even though I lost most gambling with him. They were working guys. He carries a frying pan out and said he was going to use this pan. He was going to cook the rat and eat it. The owner went crazy as he realized I saw he was using the pan he cooks all the dinners with. So think what you eat when not at home.

True story.

So I got a call from my electrician, he saw a snake in his crawl space... a BIG one. "Yea! Yea!" I think. Well it should be a little Gardener Snake. "So $675" I said. For $675 I'll catch anything. So I crawled down in the crawl space laughing to myself when I heard a "Hiss, Hiss". So I shined the light, HOLY COW... he is huge. I was terrified. "Hiss, Hiss" I heard as he was swirling around. I have glue boards so I slide them toward him. I caught him but his head was still swinging at me. So I took my trophy pictures and with a little vegetable oil, was able to release him again...

A Eastern Milk Snake.

Pretty Right!? So remember...

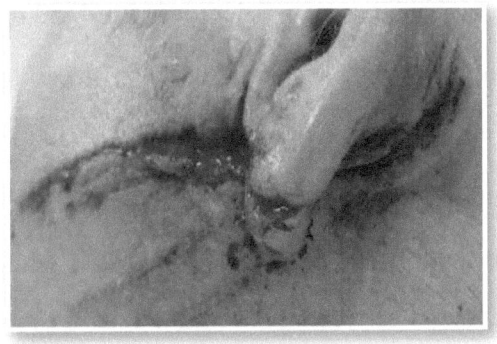

#1 - I slur my words... I was a boxer.

#2 - I had 2 Spine Surgeries

#3 - I was in 3 car accidents and fell off a roof.

I secure Bees on this lady's roof every year. Every year she is worried as I set a 32 foot ladder and go all over her roof for bees. As I climbed down, I tripped on a hose and fall face first into a broken branch of a bush standing up out of the ground. So I felt a burn and saw blood but I wanted to get paid and finish the job.

I knocked on the door and said "Can I have a Bandage?". The man freaked out, "I am calling an ambulance". I replied "No, your wife won't pay me, come hold the ladder so I can finish the job". After another hour I climbed down off the roof. I refused the ambulance again. I drove home and stopped at two places looking for a bandage to only encounter people refusing me and insisting I go to the hospital. 80 stitches later with my ear reattached, I arrive home at 1am Saturday morning. So Sunday at 8am, a customer called. "You caught 2 raccoons, come get them." So I was sore but went to the estate in Roslyn. I knocked on the door with my face in shambles. The house keeper screamed, slammed the door on me and called the police. What a 3 hour nightmare, telling the police I was not on pain killers, I had surgery and I was a boxer. Forget about it.... you had to be there to understand.

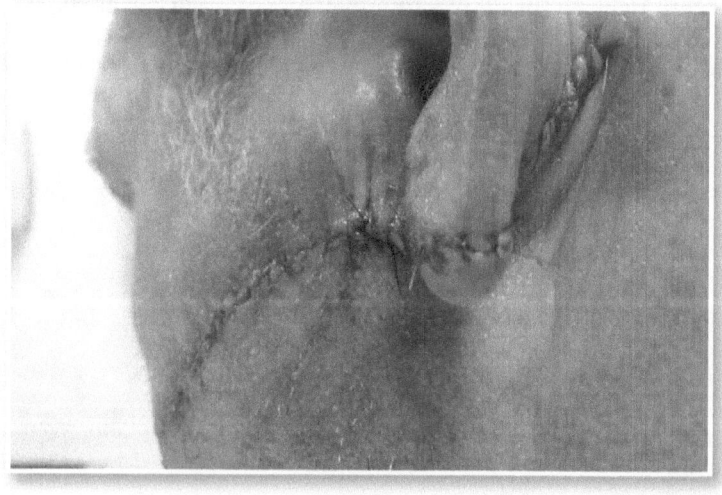

A Deer

I live on a main road so I never see a deer. At a job in Islip, while I was looking at my GPS, an animal pokes his head in my window. He scared me and I almost wet my pants. It was a deer, so I took pictures of him.

So look...How cute right? So I put water over the cage and wet him, his body all pushed up against the cage. My daughter said "Cute Doggy". I put my finger to his hair and the loudest growl, like from a lion, scared me and my daughter ran away crying.

Looks are deceiving.

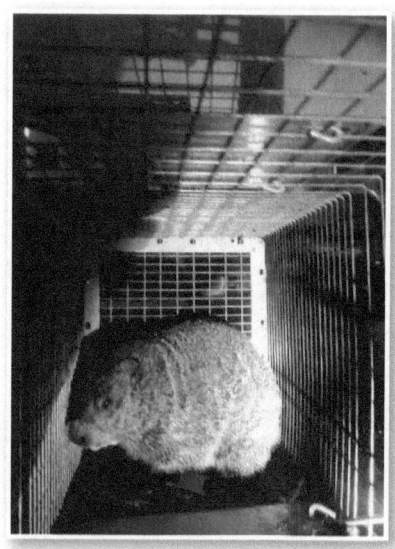

Ducks

Some people call me for crazy issues. The ducks live in his pool and when he tries to go swimming in his pool, mother duck quacks loudly and chases the homeowner out....

what does he think I am going to do?

Things are rough at home.... Had to take a kiss from any female I could...

More Pics

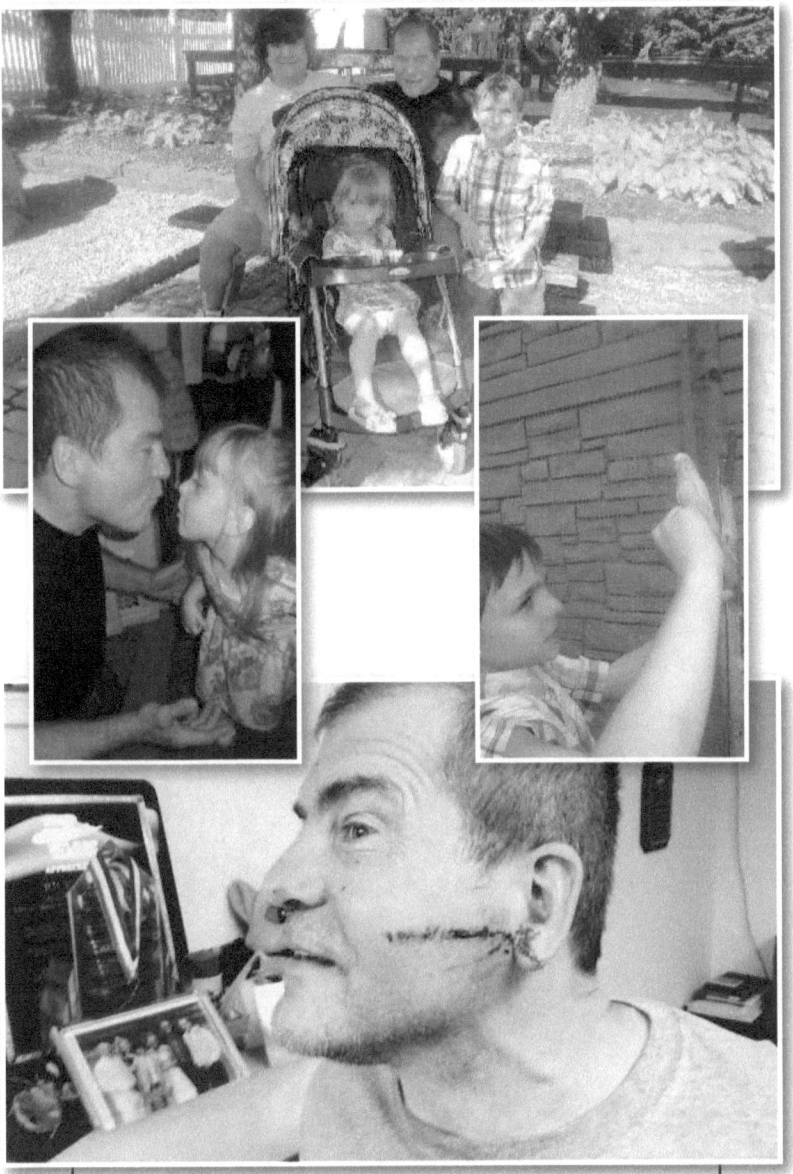

My Wife thinks I look like Frankenstein

More Pics

Devin likes his Bird Hat

More Pics

Surprised aren't you?..
Me too.

I caught Lily on a Raccoon Job 10 Years ago.

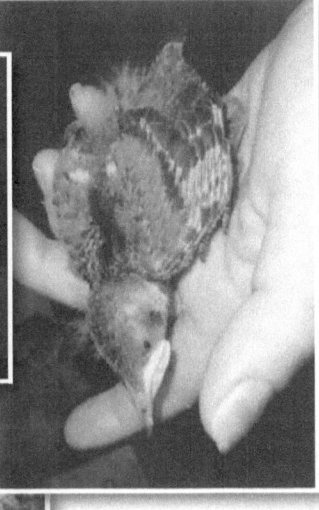

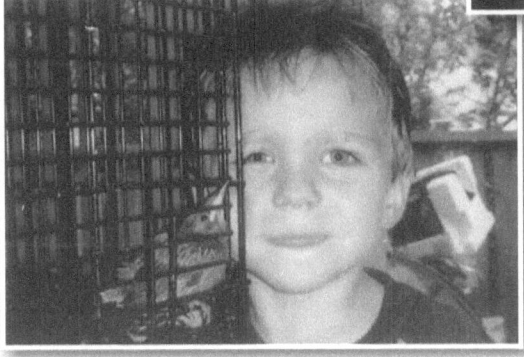

More Pics

I begged my Son to go to college but look....

Hello, I am a Woodpecker. I was stuck in an attic for 3 days pecking, yet I couldn't get out. Lenny was my hero... I am FREE now!

Even my Daughter likes the Family Business holding my rubber rat.

Hello, I am a Raccoon and this is my Dad. Everyone says we don't look alike, their crazy.... we have the same eyebrows

All of these birds flew around
my house for 6 weeks

Dad this is wierd.

Feed me again!

More Pics

Birds rub their bottoms on my carpet...wife is pissed

Pleasure but repulsed over the bird idea.

Dad, are you sure this is normal?

38

More Pics

My Living Room

Come to Daddy.

They live outside but fly to me daily to feed them.

I liked this Rat so I let him go in my neighbors yard.

More Pics

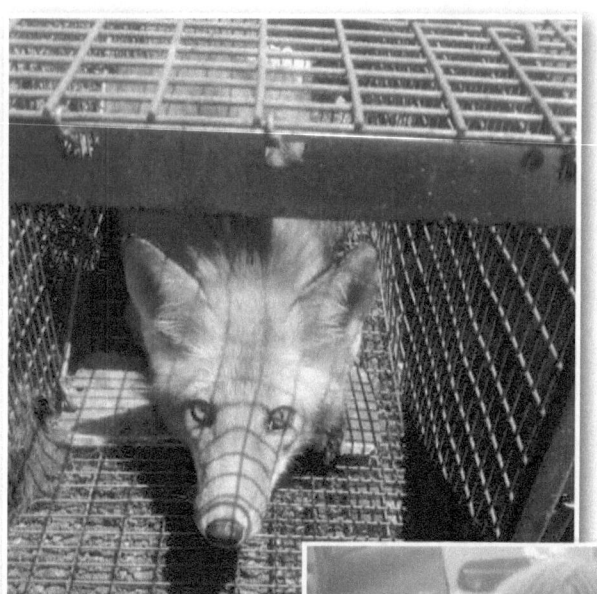

Excuse me! Yes, I am a Foxy Lady

More Pics

Baby Says "Mom, is this my bird?"

Some things NEVER change...

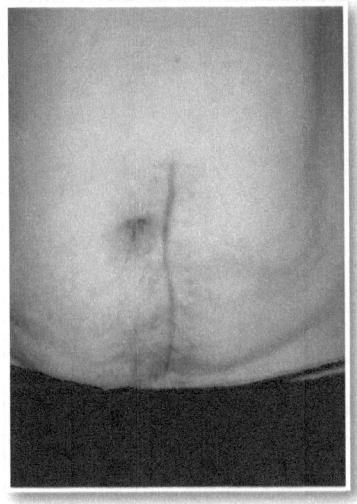

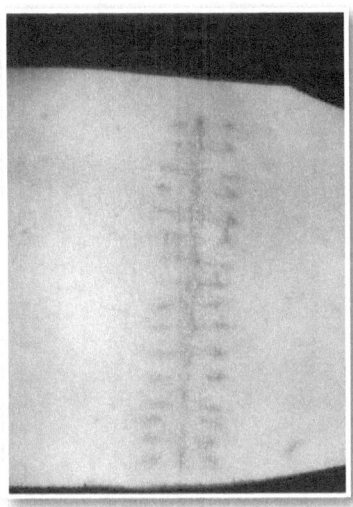

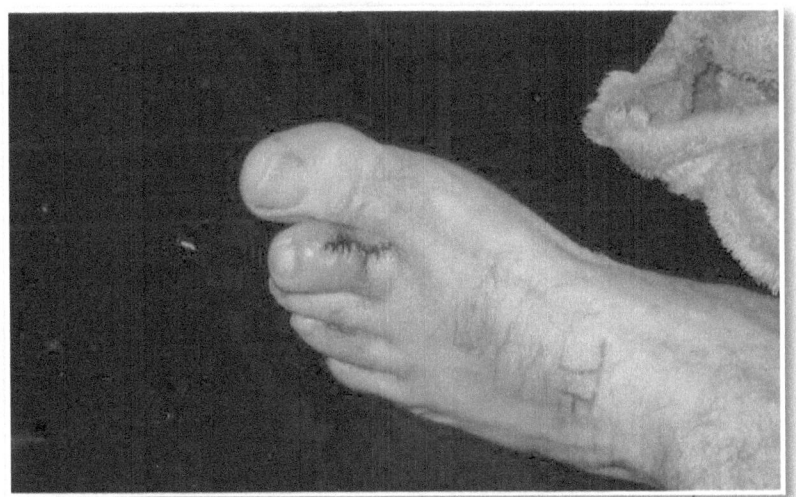

Beautiful isn't it!? Are you Hungry now?
33 Foot ladder fell on my foot and I broke a toe.

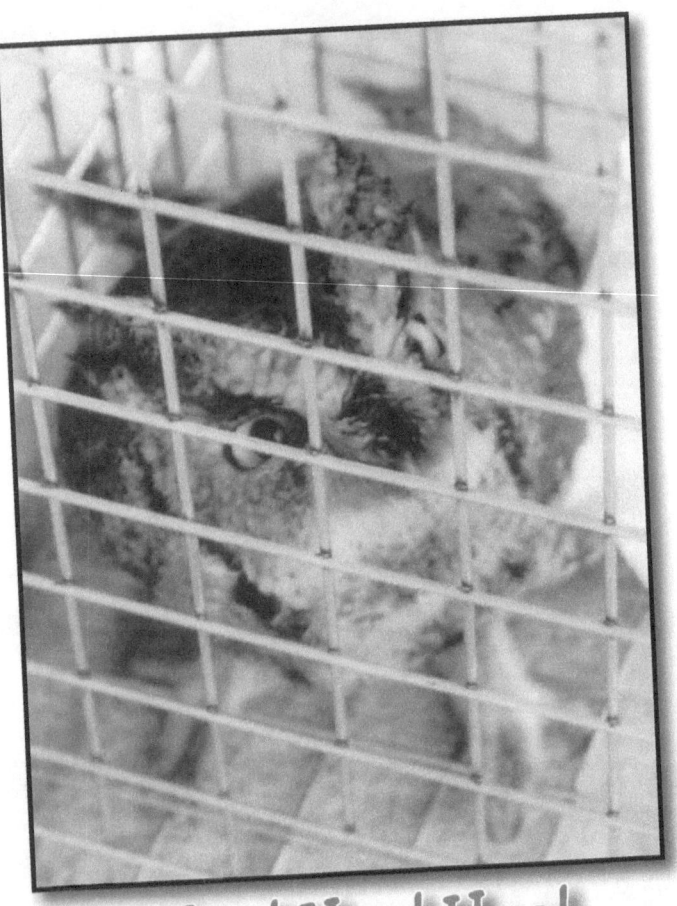

"Hoo! Hoo! Hoo!
Who put me in here...
I only had 2 Beers!"

ISBN: 0-692-45420-9
ISBN: 978-0-692-45420-6

Some stories in this book have been stretched for your entertainment.
I have 3 dogs, 1 cat, 1 ferret, 3 frogs and 2 birds - So I love wild life and
exterminate within the Department of Environmental Law.
Author: Leonard Bilski • $10.50